NO-COOK PALEO!

Kids and On The Go Cookbook

All Rights Reserved. No part of this publication may be reproduced in any form or by any means, including scanning, photocopying, or otherwise without prior written permission of the copyright holder. Copyright © 2014

Introduction

No cave bound, club wielding, hair dragging people here. Contrary to popular rumor, the Paleo way of eating is about health. Let's first say that all of the hoopla about some cave diet is just a bunch of hooey! The Paleo way of eating is simply put, a natural and healthy style of eating. Many people figure that because the Paleo style of eating limits ingredient usage that good meal ideas are hard to come by.

All kidding aside, this book was designed to make all of your friends and family think that you have Paleo super powers.

In his cook book – or shall I say cave-scripture, you will find tons of all natural, no-cooking-required, totally Paleo friendly recipes that will help you towards your health improvement goals!

Table of Contents

Paleo Cocoa Avocado Smoothie

Sunrise Piña Colada

Ginger Orange Glory

Paleo Breakfast Parfait

Spiced Cocoa Chia Pudding

Strawberry Morning Chia Pudding

Hearty Homegrown Banana Porridge

Chocolate Chia Bars

Sunshine Energy Bars

Ginger Carrot Crunch Salad

Simple Apple Almond Salad

Sunrise Berry Salad

Citrus Salad with Coconut Cream

Paleo Peach Crunch

Simple Cashew Cereal

Paleo Granola Bowl

Paleoatmeal Breakfast Bowl

Breakfast Turkey Jerky

Paleo Crêpes with Lemon Curd

Paleo Smoked Salmon Crêpes
Paleo Banana Pancake Stack
Pancakes and Berry Jam
Chocolate Breakfast Brownies
Paleo Coconut Breakfast Cakes
Paleo Carrot Cake Biscuits

Paleo Cocoa Avocado Smoothie

Prep Time: 10 minutes*

Servings: 1

INGREDIENTS

1/2 cup raw almonds

1 avocado

2 - 4 tablespoons raw cocoa powder

1/4 - 1/2 cup dried pitted dates

Water

INSTRUCTIONS

1. *Soak almonds in enough water to cover at least 6 hours, or overnight. Drain and rinse. Soak dates in enough water to cover at least 6 hours, or overnight. Drain.

2. Add soaked almonds to high-speed blender with 1 1/2 - 2 cups water. Process until well blended and almost smooth, about 1- 2 minutes.

3. Strain mixture through nut milk bag, cheesecloth or strainer back int blender.

4. Cut avocado in half and remove pit. Scoop flesh into blender with soaked dates and cocoa powder.

5. Process until smooth, about 1 minute,.

6. Pour into serving glass and serve immediately.

Sunrise Piña Colada

Prep Time: 10 minutes*
Servings: 1

INSTRUCTIONS

1 fresh coconut (or 1/2 cup flaked coconut)
1/2 cup pineapple chunks (fresh or frozen)
1 cup ice (crushed preferably)
Water

DIRECTIONS

1. *Soak flaked coconut in 1 1/2 cups water in refrigerator overnight, if using.

2. Add soaked coconut and soaking liquid to high-speed blender. Or remove flesh from fresh coconut and add to high-speed blender with 1 1/2 cups water. Process until well blended and fairly smooth, about 1 - 2 minutes.

3. Strain mixture through nut milk bag, cheesecloth or strainer back into blender.

4. Reserve pulp and set aside to dry and dehydrate, then use as coconut flour.

5. Cut pineapple flesh from peel, then chop. Add to blender with ice. Process until smooth, about 1 - 2 minutes.

6. Pour into serving glass and serve immediately.

Ginger Orange Glory

Prep Time: 5 minutes

Servings: 1

INGREDIENTS

3 oranges

1/2 grapefruit

3 large carrots

1 inch piece fresh ginger

Water (optional)

INSTRUCTIONS

1. Peel orange , grapefruit and ginger. Separate citrus segments and add to high-speed blender with carrots and ginger. Process until smooth, about 2 minutes. Add enough water to reach desired consistency.

2. Or peel and cut orange and grapefruit in half, and run through juicer with carrots and ginger.

3. Or cut orange and grapefruit in half and juice with citrus juicer. Then run carrots and ginger through juicer and add to citrus juice.

4. Pour into serving glass and serve immediately.

Paleo Breakfast Parfait

Prep Time: 10 minutes*

Servings: 2

INGREDIENTS

1/2 cup raw walnuts

1/2 cup raw almonds

1/4 cup raw pumpkin seeds

1/4 cup raw sunflower seeds

1/4 cup raw flax seeds

1 cup blueberries

1 cup raspberries

Vanilla Cream

1 cup raw cashews

2 tablespoons raw honey (or dried pitted dates)

1/2 teaspoon vanilla

1/8 teaspoon Celtic sea salt

Water

INSTRUCTIONS

1. *Soak cashews and dates (if using) in enough water to cover at least 6 hours, or overnight in refrigerator. Drain and set aside.

2. Add walnuts, almonds, pumpkin, sunflower and flax seeds to food processor or high-speed blender. Pulse to coarsely chop. Set aside.

3. For *Vanilla Cream*, add soaked cashews, honey or dates, vanilla and salt to clean food processor or high-speed blender. Process until

smooth, about 1 - 2 minutes. Add enough water or nut milk to reach desired consistency.

4. Spoon layer of fruit into serving dish. Top with chopped nuts. Spoon on layer of *Vanilla Cream*. Add second layer of chopped nuts. Top with layer of fruit.

5. Serve immediately. Or refrigerate 20 minutes and serve chilled.

Spiced Cocoa Chia Pudding

Prep Time: 10 minutes*

Servings: 2

INGREDIENTS

- 2 coconuts (or 1 cup flaked coconut)
- dried pitted dates
- tablespoons whole chia seeds
- tablespoons cocoa powder
- 1/2 teaspoon vanilla
- 1/2 teaspoon ground black pepper
- inch cayenne pepper
- inch chili powder
- inch smoked paprika
- Water

INSTRUCTIONS

1. *Soak flaked coconut in 2 cups water overnight in refrigerator, if using. Soak dates in enough water to cover at least 4 hours, or overnight in refrigerator. Drain dates.

2. Add soaked coconut and soaking liquid to high-speed blender. Or remove flesh from fresh coconuts and add to high-speed blender with 2 cups water. Process until well blended and fairly smooth, about 1 - 2 minutes.

3. Strain mixture through nut milk bag, cheesecloth or strainer back into blender.

4. Reserve pulp and set aside to dry and dehydrate, then use as coconut flour.

5. Add dates, cocoa, vanilla and spices to blender. Process until smooth about 1 minute.

6. Pour mixture into serving dish and stir in chia seeds. Set aside to thicken, about 1 minute.

7. Serve immediately. Or refrigerate 20 minutes and serve chilled.

Strawberry Morning Chia Pudding

Prep Time: 10 minutes*

Servings: 2

INGREDIENTS

2 coconuts (or 1 cup flaked coconut)

2 - 4 tablespoons raw honey (or dried pitted dates)

1/4 cup tablespoons whole chia seeds

1 cup strawberries (fresh or frozen and thawed, chopped)

1/2 teaspoon vanilla

Water

INSTRUCTIONS

1. *Soak flaked coconut in 2 cups water overnight in refrigerator, if using. Soak dates in enough water to cover at least 4 hours, or overnight in refrigerator, if using. Drain dates.

2. Add soaked coconut and soaking liquid to high-speed blender. Or remove flesh from fresh coconuts and add to high-speed blender with 2 cups water. Process until well blended and fairly smooth, about 1 - 2 minutes.

3. Strain mixture through nut milk bag, cheesecloth or strainer back into blender.

4. Reserve pulp and set aside to dry and dehydrate, then use as coconut flour.

5. Remove stems from strawberries, then cut in half. Add to blender with honey or dates, and vanilla. Process until smooth, about 1 minute.

6. Pour mixture into serving dish and stir in chia seeds. Set aside to thicken, about 1 minute.

7. Serve immediately. Or refrigerate 20 minutes and serve chilled.

Hearty Homegrown Banana Porridge

Prep Time: 10 minutes

Servings: 2

INGREDIENTS

1 coconut (1/2 cup flaked coconut)

3/4 cup raw nuts (any combination of cashews, almonds, brazil nuts, acorns, macadamia nuts, etc.)

2 overripe bananas

2 teaspoons ground cinnamon

1/4 teaspoon vanilla

1/4 teaspoon Celtic sea salt

Water

INSTRUCTIONS

1. * Soak nuts in enough water to cover for at least 6 hours, or overnight in refrigerator. Drain and rinse, then set aside. Soak flaked coconut in 2 cups water in refrigerator overnight, if using.

2. Add soaked coconut and soaking liquid to high-speed blender. Or remove flesh from fresh coconut and add to high-speed blender with 2 cups water. Process until well blended and fairly smooth, about 1 - 2 minutes.

3. Strain mixture through nut milk bag, cheesecloth or strainer back into blender or food processor.

4. Reserve pulp and set aside to dry and dehydrate, then use as coconut flour.

5. Peel bananas and add to processor with vanilla, salt and 1 teaspoon cinnamon. Process until thick and mostly smooth, about 1 minute.

6. Transfer to serving dish and serve immediately.

Chocolate Chia Bars

Prep Time: 25 minutes
Servings: 6

INGREDIENTS

1 cup dried pitted dates
1/4 cup raw nuts (any combination of cashews, almonds, brazil nuts, acorns, macadamia nuts, etc.)
1 tablespoon raw cocoa powder
2 tablespoons chia seeds
1/2 teaspoon ground cinnamon
1/2 teaspoon vanilla
1 inch ground black pepper
1 inch Celtic sea salt
1/3 cup warm water

INSTRUCTIONS

1. Soak dates in warm water 5 - 10 minutes, then drain.

2. Line loaf pan with parchment paper.

3. Add nuts to food processor or high-speed blender with soaked dates, cocoa, cinnamon, vanilla, salt and pepper. Process for about 1 minute, until dates and nuts break down and mixture sticks together when pressed.

4. Transfer mixture to small mixing bowl and add chia seeds. Mix with large spoon until well combined, about 1 minute.

5. Transfer mixture to prepared loaf pan and press firmly into bottom with hands or spatula.

6. Place in refrigerator and chill for 10 minutes. Then remove and cut into 6 bars.

7. Serve immediately. Or store in refrigerator up to 2 weeks.

Sunshine Energy Bars

Prep Time: 25 minutes

Servings: 6

INGREDIENTS

3/4 cup dried apricots

3/4 cup dried mango slices

1 1/4 cup raw nuts (any combination of cashews, almonds, brazil nuts, acorns, macadamia nuts, etc.)

1/2 teaspoon ground ginger

1/4 teaspoon vanilla

1/3 cup warm water

1 lemon

INSTRUCTIONS

1. Juice lemon and add to bowl with warm water and fruit. Soak 5 - 10 minutes, then drain.

2. Line loaf pan with parchment paper.

3. Add nuts to food processor or high-speed blender with soaked fruit, ginger and vanilla. Process for about 1 minute, until fruit and nuts break down and mixture sticks together when pressed.

4. Transfer mixture to prepared loaf pan and press firmly into bottom with hands or spatula.

5. Place in refrigerator and chill for 10 minutes. Then remove and cut into 6 bars.

6. Serve immediately. Or store in refrigerator up to 2 weeks.

Ginger Carrot Crunch Salad

Prep Time: 5 minutes

Servings: 1

INSTRUCTIONS

2 large carrots

3 tablespoon dried cranberries

1/4 cup raw almonds

1/2 small orange (or tangerine)

1/2 piece fresh ginger

1/2 teaspoon ground ginger

DIRECTIONS

1. Add carrots to food processor with shredding attachment and process, or grate with grater. Add to medium mixing bowl with cranberries and ground ginger.

2. Add almonds to food processor and pulse to coarsely chop. Or add to paper or plastic kitchen bag and pound with heavy rolling pin to crush. Peel ginger and dice or finely grate. Zest *then* juice orange. Add to carrot mixture and toss to combine.

3. Transfer to serving dish and serve immediately. Or refrigerate 20 minutes and serve chilled.

Simple Apple Almond Salad

Prep Time: 5 minutes

Servings: 1

INSTRUCTIONS

1 apple

1 small banana

1/4 cup blueberries

1/4 cup raw almonds

2 dried pitted dates

2 tablespoons pomegranate seeds (or dried goji or noni berries)

1/4 teaspoon ground cinnamon

INGREDIENTS

1. Core and dice apple. Peel and dice banana. Add to serving dish and mix to combine. Top with blueberries.

2. Chop almonds and dates. Or add to food processor and pulse to coarsely grind.

3. Top fruit with chopped nuts and dates. Sprinkle with pomegranate seeds and cinnamon and serve immediately.

Sunrise Berry Salad

Prep Time: 10 minutes

Servings: 1

INSTRUCTIONS

1 nectarine

1/2 cup strawberries

1/4 cup blackberries

1/4 cup blueberry

1/4 cup cherries

1/4 cup raw nuts (cashews, almonds, brazil nuts, acorns, macadamia, etc.)

1/2 inch piece fresh ginger

small sprig fresh mint

INGREDIENTS

1. Cut nectarine in half and remove pit. Dice and add to small mixing bowl. Remove stems from strawberries and quarter. Pit cherries. Add to bowl with blackberries and blueberries.

2. Peel ginger and mince or finely grate. Chiffon mint leaves. Add to bowl and toss to combine. Transfer to serving dish.

3. Add nuts to food processor and pulse to coarsely chop. Or add to paper or plastic kitchen bag and pound with heavy rolling pin to crush.

4. Sprinkle on nuts and serve immediately. Or refrigerate 20 minutes and serve chilled.

Citrus Salad with Coconut Cream

Prep Time: 10 minutes

Servings: 1

INSTRUCTIONS

1 fresh coconut (or 1/2 cup flaked coconut)

1/4 - 1/3 cup dried pitted dates (or raw honey)

1 blood orange

1 tangerine (or navel orange or clementine)

1/2 grapefruit (ruby red, pink or white)

1/2 lime

1 tablespoon sunflower seeds (optional)

Water

INGREDIENTS

1. *Soak flaked coconut in 1 cup water overnight in refrigerator, if using. Soak dates in enough water to cover overnight in refrigerator. Drain.

2. Add soaked coconut and soaking liquid to high-speed blender. Or remove flesh from fresh coconut and add to high-speed blender with 3/4 cup water. Process until thick and fairly smooth, about 1 - 2 minutes.

3. Strain mixture through nut milk bag, cheesecloth or strainer back int blender or to food processor.

4. Reserve pulp and set aside to dry and dehydrate, then use as coconut flour.

5. Add soaked dates or honey to processor and process until smooth. Set aside.

6. Peel all citrus and cut into segments. Add to serving dish. Top with sweet coconut cream. Sprinkle on sunflower seeds (optional).

7. Serve immediately. Or refrigerate 20 minutes and serve chilled.

Paleo Peach Crunch

Prep Time: 5 minutes

Servings: 1

INGREDIENTS

2 ripe peaches (or nectarines)

4 dried pitted dates

1/3 cup raw almonds

1/4 teaspoon ground cinnamon

1/4 teaspoon ground ginger

1/8 teaspoon vanilla

1/8 teaspoon ground white pepper (or ground black pepper)

INSTRUCTIONS

1. Add dates, almonds vanilla and spices to food processor or high-speed blender. Pulse to coarsely grind, about 1 minute.

2. Cut peaches in half and remove pits. Dice peaches and transfer to serving dish.

3. Sprinkle on almond mixture and serve immediately.

Simple Cashew Cereal

Prep Time: 5 minutes*

Servings: 1

INGREDIENTS

1 1/2 cups raw cashews

1 banana

1/4 cup blueberries

1 tablespoon raw honey (or 2 pitted dates)

1 tablespoon lemon juice

1/4 teaspoon vanilla

1/4 teaspoon Celtic sea salt

Water

INSTRUCTIONS

1. *Soak cashews and dates (if using) in enough water to cover overnight in refrigerator. Drain.

2. Peel banana. Add to food processor or high-speed blender with soaked cashews, dates or honey, lemon juice, vanilla and salt. Process until thick and fairly smooth, about 1 - 2 minutes. Add enough water to reach desired consistency.

3. Transfer to serving dish and top with blueberries. Serve immediately.

Paleo Granola Bowl

Prep Time: 10 minutes*

Servings: 1

INGREDIENTS

3/4 cup raw almonds

1/3 cups raw walnuts

1/3 cups cashews

1/4 cup raw pumpkin seeds

1/4 cup shredded or flaked coconut

2 tablespoon dried cranberries

1/3 cup dried pitted dates

1/4 tablespoon vanilla

1/4 tablespoon cinnamon

1/4 teaspoon ground ginger

1/2 teaspoon Celtic sea salt

Water

INSTRUCTIONS

1. *Separately oak 1/4 cup almonds in enough water to cover at least 6 hours, or overnight. Drain and rinse. Soak 1/4 cupdates in enough water to cover at least 6 hours, or overnight. Drain.

2. Add soaked almonds to high-speed blender with 2/3 - 3/4 cup water. Process until well blended and almost smooth, about 1- 2 minutes.

3. Strain mixture through nut milk bag, cheesecloth or strainer back into blender.

4. Add soaked dates to blender with vanilla, salt and ginger. Process until smooth, about 1 minutes. Add to medium mixing bowl.

5. Chop remaining almonds, walnuts and dates by hand. Or add to clean food processor or high-speed blender and pulse to roughly chop. Add to bowl with pumpkin seeds, flaked coconut, cranberries and cinnamon. Mix to combine.

6. Transfer to serving dish and serve immediately. Or refrigerate 20 minutes and serve chilled.

Paleoatmeal Breakfast Bowl

Prep Time: 5 minutes*

Servings: 2

INGREDIENTS

2 cage free eggs (optional)

1/2 apple

1/4 cup flaked or shredded coconut

1/4 - 1/3 cup dried pitted dates

1/3 cup raw walnuts

1/3 cup raw almonds

2 tablespoons coconut oil (or coconut butter or cacao butter)

2 tablespoons flax seed (or chia seed)

2 tablespoons raisins

2 tablespoons dried goji berries (optional)

1 teaspoon ground cinnamon

Pinch Celtic sea salt

Water

INSTRUCTIONS

1. *Soak walnuts and almonds in enough water to cover for at least 6 hours, or overnight in refrigerator. Drain and rinse, then set aside. Soak dates in enough water to cover for at least 6 hours, or overnight in refrigerator. Drain and set aside. Soak flaked coconut in 1 cup water overnight in refrigerator.

2. Add flax or chia to food processor or high-speed blender and process until finely ground. Add coconut oil and process until thick paste forms.

3. Add dates, nuts, eggs, cinnamon, salt, soaked coconut and soaking liquid to processor. Process until thick mixture forms, about 1 - 2 minutes. Transfer to serving dish.

4. Core and dice apple. Top with dices apple, raisins and goji berries (optional).

5. Serve immediately.

Breakfast Turkey Jerky

Prep Time: 10 minutes*

Dehydrating Time: 4 - 8 hours

Servings: 4

INGREDIENTS

4 oz organic turkey (dark meat)

2 tablespoons coconut aminos (or liquid aminos)

2 tablespoons tamari (or liquid aminos or coconut aminos)

1 tablespoon lemon juice (or raw apple cider vinegar)

1 tablespoons Celtic sea salt

1/2 teaspoon garlic powder

1/2 teaspoon onion powder

1/2 teaspoon smoked paprika

Pinch cayenne pepper

INSTRUCTIONS

1. Prepare two sheet parchment. Lay one on cutting board.

2. Cut turkey into 1/4 inch strips and lay in single layer on parchment. Pound with tenderizing side of kitchen mallet. Cover turkey with second parchment sheet, then pound with flat side of tenderizing mallet to 1/8 inch thickness.

3. *Place turkey strips in medium mixing bowl or shallow dish. Add coconut aminos, tamari, lemon juice, salt and spices. Mix well to coat. Cover and place in refrigerator for 8 hours, or overnight.

4. Remove turkey from refrigerator and lay in single layer on dehydrator trays. Place trays in dehydrator and set to 120 degrees F for 4 - 8 hours.

5. After 4 hours dehydrating time, remove trays from dehydrator and test turkey by bending. If it cracks, remove and serve immediately. Or store in airtight container.

6. If still flexible, place back in dehydrator and continue dehydrating up to 4 hours, or until desired texture is achieved.

Paleo Crêpes with Lemon Curd

Prep Time: 15 minutes*

Dehydrating Time: 7 - 10 hours

Servings: 2

INGREDIENTS

Crêpes

1 young coconut (plus coconut water)

1/2 orange

1/2 cup flax seeds

1 tablespoon raw honey (or dried pitted dates)

1 teaspoon ground cinnamon

Lemon Curd

1/3 cup raw cashews

1/4 cup coconut butter(or cacao butter)

2 lemons (1/4 cup juice)

2 - 4 tablespoons raw honey

Pinch Celtic sea salt

Pinch of turmeric (optional)

Water

INSTRUCTIONS

1. For *Crêpes*, add flax to food processor or high-speed blender. Process until finely ground, up to 5 minutes.

2. Remove flesh and water from young coconut. Peel orange and cut into segments. Add to processor with honey and cinnamon. Process until thick and smooth, about 1 - 2 minutes.

3. Place parchment paper or dehydrator sheets on dehydrator trays.

4. Spread batter on prepared sheets. Place trays in dehydrator and set to 115 degrees F for 6 - 8 hours.

5. Remove trays from dehydrator. Remove *Crêpes* from parchment or dehydrator liners, flip, and place directly on dehydrator tray. Place trays back in dehydrator and continue dehydrating 1 - 2 hours, until surface is dry but *Crêpe* is still pliable.

6. Remove from dehydrator and cut into desired shape and size. Set aside.

7. *For *Lemon Curd*, soak cashews in enough water to cover for at least 6 hours, or overnight in refrigerator. Drain and rinse.

8. Zest 1 lemon, then juice lemons into food processor or high-speed blender. Add coconut butter, honey, salt and turmeric, for color (optional).Process until smooth, about 1 - 2 minutes. Add enough water to reach desired consistency.

9. Lay *Crêpes* flat and top with line of *Lemon Curd* down center. Roll up *Crêpes* and transfer to serving dish. Serve immediately.

Paleo Smoked Salmon Crêpes

Prep Time: 10 minutes

Dehydrating Time: 7 - 10 hours

Servings: 2

INGREDIENTS

4 - 6 oz smoked salmon

1 ripe avocado

1/2 lemon

1 sprig fresh dill

1 teaspoon sesame seeds (black or white)

Crêpes

1 young coconut (plus coconut water)

1/3 cup raw sunflower seeds

1/2 cup flax seeds

1/2 white ground pepper (or 1/4 teaspoon ground black pepper)

1/2 teaspoon Celtic sea salt

Water

INSTRUCTIONS

1. For *Crêpes*, add flax to food processor or high-speed blender. Process until finely ground, up to 5 minutes. Add sunflower seeds and process until finely ground, about 1 minute.

2. Remove flesh and water from young coconut. Add to processor with salt and pepper. Process until smooth batter forms, about 1 - 2 minutes. Add enough water to reach desired consistency.

3. Place parchment paper or dehydrator sheets on dehydrator trays.

4. Spread batter on prepared sheets. Place trays in dehydrator and set to 115 degrees F for 6 - 8 hours.

5. Remove trays from dehydrator. Remove *Crêpes* from parchment or dehydrator liners, flip, and place directly on dehydrator tray. Place trays back in dehydrator and continue dehydrating 1 - 2 hours, until surface is dry but *Crêpe* is still pliable.

6. Remove from dehydrator and cut into desired shape and size. Set aside.

7. Finely chop fresh dill. Cut avocado in half and remove pit. Slice flesh in peel.

8. Lay *Crêpes* flat and top with line of smoked salmon down center. Scoop portion of sliced avocado over smoked salmon. Sprinkle on chopped dill. Roll up *Crêpes* and transfer to serving dish.

9. Top *Crêpes* with squeeze of lemon juice and sprinkle on sesame seeds. Serve immediately.

Paleo Banana Pancake Stack

Prep Time: 15 minutes

Dehydrating Time: 8 - 9 hours

Servings: 2

INGREDIENTS

Banana Pancakes

2 overripe bananas

1/2 cup raw cashews (or 1/4 cup raw cashew butter)

1/4 cup flax seed

1 teaspoon ground cinnamon

1/2 teaspoon vanilla

1/2 teaspoon cardamom (optional)

Water

Topping

1 ripe banana

1/4 teaspoon ground cinnamon

1 tablespoon raw honey (or date butter)

INSTRUCTIONS

1. For *Banana Pancakes*, add flax to food processor or high-speed blender. Process until finely ground, about 2 minutes.

2. Add cashews to processor, if using. Process until smooth, up to 5 minutes.

3. Or add cashew butter to processor with bananas, cinnamon, vanilla and cardamom (optional). Process until smooth batter forms, about 1 - 2 minutes. Add enough water to reach desired consistency.

4. Place parchment paper or dehydrator sheets on dehydrator trays.

5. Use spoon to spread batter on prepared sheets in 2 x 2 inch circles 1/4 inch thick. Place trays in dehydrator and set to 110 degrees F for 6 hours.

6. Remove trays from dehydrator. Flip *Banana Pancakes* and place trays back in dehydrator. Continue dehydrating 2 - 3 hours, until surface is dry but *Banana Pancakes* are still moist and pliable.

7. For *Topping*, peel banana and slice. Add to small mixing bowl with cinnamon and honey or date butter. Toss to coat.

8. Remove *Banana Pancakes* from dehydrator and transfer to serving dish. Top with spiced banana *Topping* and serve immediately.

Pancakes and Berry Jam

Prep Time: 15 minutes*

Dehydrating Time: 8 - 9 hours

Servings: 2

INGREDIENTS

Pancakes

1 young coconut (plus coconut water)

1/2 cup raw cashews (or 1/4 cup raw cashew butter)

1/4 cup flax seed

1/4 teaspoon ground cinnamon

1/2 teaspoon vanilla

Water

Berry Jam

1 orange

1/4 cup dried raspberries

1/4 cup dried cherries

1/4 cup dried strawberries

Water

INSTRUCTIONS

1. *Soak dried fruit in enough water to cover at least 4 hours, or overnight in refrigerator. Drain and reserve soaking liquid. Set aside.

2. For *Pancakes*, add flax to food processor or high-speed blender. Process until finely ground, about 2 minutes.

3. Add cashews to processor, if using. Process until smooth, up to 5 minutes. Or use prepared cashew butter.

4. Remove flesh and water from young coconut add and add to processor with cashew butter, cinnamon and vanilla cardamom. Process until smooth batter forms, about 1 - 2 minutes. Add enough water to reach desired consistency.

5. Place parchment paper or dehydrator sheets on dehydrator trays.

6. Use spoon to spread batter on prepared sheets in 2 x 2 inch circles 1/4 inch thick. Place trays in dehydrator and set to 110 degrees F for 6 hours.

7. Remove trays from dehydrator. Flip *Pancakes* and place trays back in dehydrator. Continue dehydrating 2 - 3 hours, until surface is dry but *Pancakes* are still moist and pliable.

8. For *Berry Jam*, zest *then* juice orange into clean food processor or high-speed blender. Add soaked fruit and process until mostly smooth, about 1 minute. Add enough soaking liquid and/or water to reach desired consistency and sweetness.

9. Remove *Pancakes* from dehydrator and transfer to serving dish. Top with *Berry Jam* and serve immediately.

Chocolate Breakfast Brownies

Prep Time: 10 minutes

Servings: 2

INGREDIENTS

1 cup dried pitted dates

1/2 cup cashews

1/2 cup sunflower seeds

1/4 cup hulled hemp seeds (or chia or flax seeds)

1/4 cup shredded or flaked coconut

1/4 cup raw cocoa powder

2 tablespoons coconut oil (or coconut butter or cacao butter)

1 teaspoon vanilla

1/4 teaspoon Celtic sea salt

Pinch ground black pepper.

1/4 cup raw cacao nibs (or dried goji berries, noni berries, pomegranates seeds, or any combination)

INSTRUCTIONS

1. Add hemp, chia or flax seeds sunflower seeds to food processor or high-speed blender. Process until finely ground, about 2 minutes. Add sunflower seeds and process until finely ground, about 1 minute Add cashews and process until finely ground, about 1 minute.

2. Add dates in batches and continue processing until mixture is well ground and sticks together.

3. Add coconut, cocoa , coconut oil, vanilla, salt and pepper. Process about 30 seconds to incorporate.

4. Transfer to medium mixing bowl and add cacao nibs, dried berries or pomegranate seeds. Mix to combine.

5. Transfer mixture to lined loaf pan and press into bottom with hands or spatula. Slice and serve. Or refrigerate 20 minutes to firm, then slice and serve.

Paleo Coconut Breakfast Cakes

Prep Time: 10 minutes*

Servings: 2

INGREDIENTS

Coconut Breakfast Cake

1 fresh coconut (or 1/2 cup flaked or shredded coconut)

1/2 cup ground flax seed (or chia seed)

1/4 cup raw honey (or 1/3 cup dried pitted dates)

2 tablespoons coconut oil (or coconut butter or cacao butter)

1/2 teaspoon ground cinnamon

1/4 teaspoon Celtic sea salt

Water

Apricot Jam

1 cup dried apricots

2 tablespoons lemon juice

1/4 inch piece fresh ginger (or 1/2 teaspoon ground ginger)

Water

INSTRUCTIONS

1. *For *Coconut Breakfast Cakes*, soak flaked coconut and in 1 cup water overnight in refrigerator, if using. Soak dates in enough water to cover overnight in refrigerator, if using. Drain.

2. Add soaked coconut and soaking liquid to high-speed blender. Or remove flesh from fresh coconut and add to high-speed blender with 1 cup water, ground flax or chia, soaked dates or honey, coconut oil,

salt and cinnamon. Pulse to coarsely grind, until mixture sticks together.

3. Form mixture into 6 balls and flatten into cakes. Or mold in lined muffin tins. Set aside.

4. For *Apricot Jam*, peel ginger and add to clean food processor or high-speed blender with apricots and lemon juice. Process until smooth, about 1 minute. Add enough water to reach desired consistency.

5. Transfer *Coconut Breakfast Cakes* to serving dish. Top with *Apricot Jam* and serve immediately. Or refrigerate 20 minutes and serve chilled.

Paleo Carrot Cake Biscuits

Prep Time: 20 minutes

Servings: 6

INGREDIENTS

Carrot Biscuit

3 large carrots (1 1/2 cups shredded)

1/3 - 1/2 cup dried pitted dates

1/2 cup raw walnuts

1/3 cup shredded or flaked coconut

1/4 cup raisins (optional)

1/2 teaspoon ground cinnamon

1/2 teaspoon ground ginger

1/4 teaspoon Celtic sea salt

Pinch ground nutmeg

Pinch ground black pepper

Sweet Tahini

1 cup raw sesame seeds (or 1/2 cup raw tahini)

1/4 cup raw pitted dates (or 3 tablespoon raw honey)

1 tablespoon lemon juice

INSTRUCTIONS

1. For *Carrot Biscuit*, add carrots, dates, walnuts, coconut, salt and spices to food processor or high-speed blender. Pulse to coarsely grind, until mixture sticks together.

2. Transfer to small mixing bowl and stir in raisins (optional).

3. Form mixture into 6 balls and flatten into biscuits. Or mold in lined muffin tins. Set aside.

4. For *Sweet Tahini*, add raw sesame seeds to clean food processor or high-speed blender and process until smooth, up to 5 minutes. Add dates or honey and lemon juice.

5. Or add prepared tahini to clean food processor or high-speed blender with dates or raw honey and lemon juice. Process until smooth, about 1 - 2 minutes.

6. Transfer *Carrot Biscuits* to serving dish. Top with *Sweet Tahini* and serve immediately. Or refrigerate 20 minutes and serve chilled.

On The Go Cookbook

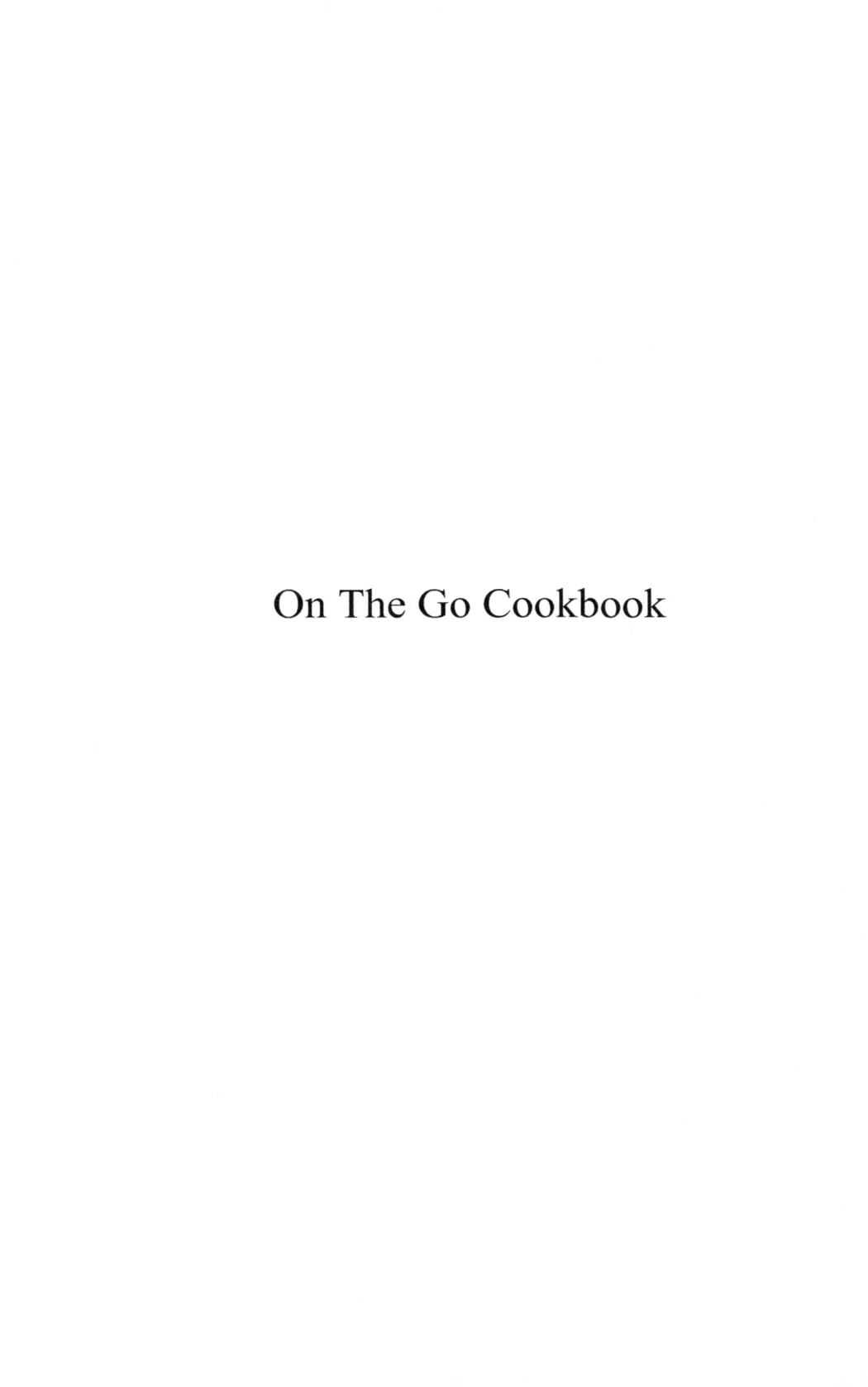

Table of Contents

Sunrise Lemon Bars
Ginger Snaps
Paleo Cocoa Cookies
Primal Trail Mix
Homemade Beef Jerky
Apricot Pockets
Primal Blondie Bars
Spiced Sweet Bread
Lemon Coconut Biscuits
Spiced Sesame Chips
Cheesy Kale Flax Crackers
Breaded Jalapeño Bites
Stuffed Pepperdew Poppers
Berry Granola Bars
Banana Strawberry Leather
Carrot Crisps
Crisp Acorn Squash Chips
Beet Chip Medley
Dried Mango
Primal Pineapple Strips
Crisp Banana Chips
Crisp Apple Chips
Spiced Kale Chips

Sweet Potato Crisps
Cheesy Veggie Popcorn

Sunrise Lemon Bars

Prep Time: 25 minutes

Servings: 6

INGREDIENTS

1 cup raw cashews

2 lemons

1/2 cup dried pineapple

1/2 cup flaked or shredded coconut

1/4 cup dried apricots

1/4 teaspoon ground ginger

1/4 teaspoon vanilla

Pinch Celtic sea salt

1/3 cup warm water

INSTRUCTIONS

1. Zest *then* juice lemons into small mixing bowl. Reserve half of juice and zest.
2. Soak dried pineapple and apricots in warm water and juice and zest of 1 lemon for 5 - 10 minutes.
3. Line loaf pan with parchment paper.
4. Add cashews to food processor or high-speed blender. Drain fruit and add to processor with coconut, salt, spices, and lemon juice and zest. Process for about 1 minute, until fruit and nuts break down and mixture sticks together when pressed.
5. Transfer mixture to prepared loaf pan and press firmly into bottom with hands or spatula.

6. Place in refrigerator and chill for 10 minutes. Remove and cut into 6 bars.
7. Serve immediately. Or store refrigerated in airtight container up to 2 weeks.

Ginger Snaps

Prep Time: 5 minutes
Dehydrating Time: 4 - 8 hours
Servings: 12

INGREDIENTS

- cups raw almond flour
- 1/2 cups dried pitted dates
- inch piece fresh ginger
- tablespoons raw coconut oil (or raw cacao or coconut butter)
- tablespoons raw honey
- teaspoons ground ginger
- teaspoons ground cinnamon
- 1/2 teaspoon ground black pepper (or ground white pepper)
- 1/2 teaspoon vanilla
- 1/4 teaspoon Celtic sea salt

INSTRUCTIONS

1. Peel and grate ginger. Add to food processor or high-speed blender with almond flour, dates, oil or butter, honey, salt and spices . Process until mixture is well ground and comes together, about 2 minutes.
2. Line dehydrator trays with dehydrator or parchment sheets.
3. Form mixture into 12 - 24 balls and place on lined dehydrator trays. Press to flatten.
4. Place in dehydrator and dehydrate at 115 degrees F for 4 - 8 hours, until desired crispiness is reached.

5. Remove from dehydrator and transfer to serving dish. Serve immediately. Or store in airtight container.

Paleo Cocoa Cookies

Prep Time: 10 minutes*

Dehydrating Time: 8 - 16 hours

Servings: 12

INGREDIENTS

1/2 cup almonds

3/4 cups cashews

1/3 cup dates

1/4 cup raw cocoa powder

1 tablespoon raw oil (coconut, walnut, almond, sesame, etc.)

1 teaspoon vanilla

1/4 teaspoon Celtic sea salt

Water

INSTRUCTIONS

1. *Soak almonds in enough water to cover for at least 6 hours, or overnight in refrigerator. Drain and rinse. Soak cashews and dates in enough water to cover for at least 1 hour. Drain.
2. Add soaked almonds and cashews to food processor or high-speed blender. Process until finely ground, about 1 - 2 minutes.
3. Add dates, cocoa, oil, vanilla and salt to processor. Process until mixture is well combined and sticks together, about 1 - 2 minutes.
4. Line dehydrator trays with dehydrator or parchment sheets.
5. Form mixture into 12 balls and place on dehydrator or parchment sheets. Press to flatten.
6. Place in dehydrator and dehydrate at 115 degrees F for about 8 - 16 hours, depending on desired crispiness.

7. Remove from dehydrator and transfer to serving dish. Serve immediately. Or store in airtight container.

Primal Trail Mix

Prep Time: 5 minutes

Servings: 4

INGREDIENTS

1/2 cup raw almonds

1/2 cup raw pumpkin seeds

1/2 cup cashews

1/4 cup golden raisins

1/4 cup dried blueberries

1/4 cup dried strawberries

INSTRUCTIONS

1. Roughly chop dried strawberries. Add to medium mixing bowl with fruit and nuts. Mix to combine.
2. Transfer to serving dish and serve immediately. Or store in airtight container.

Homemade Beef Jerky

Prep Time: 10 minutes*

Dehydrating Time: 4 - 8 hours

Servings: 4

INGREDIENTS

4 oz grass-fed beef

2 tablespoons coconut aminos (or liquid aminos or tamari)

2 tablespoons lemon juice (or raw apple cider vinegar)

1 tablespoons Celtic sea salt

1/2 teaspoon ground ginger

1/2 teaspoon garlic powder

1/2 teaspoon onion powder

1/2 teaspoon smoked paprika

1/2 teaspoon cayenne pepper

INSTRUCTIONS

1. Prepare two parchment sheets. Lay one on cutting board.
2. Cut slice beef into 1/4 inch strips and lay in single layer on parchment. Pound with tenderizing side of kitchen mallet. Cover beef with second parchment sheet, then pound with flat side of tenderizing mallet to 1/8 inch thickness.
3. *Place beef strips in medium mixing bowl or shallow dish. Add coconut aminos, lemon juice, salt and spices. Mix well to coat. Cover and place in refrigerator for 8 hours, or overnight.
4. Remove beef from refrigerator and lay in single layer on dehydrator trays. Place in dehydrator and dehydrate at 120 degrees F for 4 - 8 hours.

5. After 4 hours dehydrating time, remove trays from dehydrator and test beef by bending. If it cracks, remove and serve immediately. Or store in airtight container.
6. If still flexible, place back in dehydrator and continue dehydrating up to 4 hours, or until desired texture is achieved.

Apricot Pockets

Prep Time: 10 minutes

Servings: 4

INGREDIENTS

1 cup dried apricots

1/4 cup raw cashews

2 - 3 tablespoons dried cranberries

2 - 3 tablespoons dried blueberries

INSTRUCTIONS

1. Roughly chop cashews and add too small mixing bowl with cranberries and blueberries. Mix to combine.
2. Open apricots slightly to reveal pocket. Take pinch of mixed nuts and fruit and stuff apricots. Leave a little room to pinch apricot closed.
3. Transfer to serving dish and serve immediately. Or store in airtight container.

Primal Blondie Bars

Prep Time: 35 minutes

Servings: 6

INGREDIENTS

1 cup dried pitted dates

1 cup flaked or shredded coconut

3/4 cup golden flax seed

1/2 cup raw sunflower seeds (or raw pine nuts)

1/4 cup cacao butter (or coconut butter)

1/4 teaspoon Celtic sea salt

1 teaspoon vanilla

1/4 cup cacao nibs (or raw chocolate chunks) (optional)

INSTRUCTIONS

1. Line baking dish with parchment paper. Allow cacao butter or coconut butter to soften.
2. Add flax to food processor or high-speed blender and process until finely ground, about 2 minutes. Add sunflower seeds and cacao butter. Process until fairly smooth, about 2 minutes.
3. Add dates, coconut, vanilla and salt. Process until mixture comes together, about 1 minute.
4. Transfer to medium mixing bowl and stir in cacao nibs or raw chocolate chunks (optional).
5. Transfer mixture to lined dish and press into bottom with hands or spatula. Place in freezer at least 25 minutes.
6. Remove from freezer. Slice and serve chilled. Or allow to warm slightly and serve.

Spiced Sweet Bread

Prep Time: 10 minutes

Dehydrating Time: 6 - 8 hours

Servings: 8

INGREDIENTS

1 apple

1 lemon

1 orange

1 cup dried pitted dates

1/2 cup dried apricots

1/3 cup ground flax seed

1/2 cup raw pecans

1/2 cup raw walnuts

1 teaspoon ground cinnamon

1 teaspoon ground ginger

1/4 teaspoon Celtic sea salt

INSTRUCTIONS

1. Add pecans, walnuts and flax to food processor or high-speed blender. Process until finely ground, about 1 minute.
2. Peel and roughly chop apple around core. Zest *then* juice orange and lemon. Add to food processor or high-speed blender with dates, apricots, cinnamon, ginger and salt. Process until mixture is well ground and sticks together, about 2 minutes.
3. Line dehydrator tray with dehydrator or parchment sheet.
4. Form mixture into 2 loaves and place on lined dehydrator tray. Place in dehydrator and dehydrate at 115 degrees F for 2 hours.

Reduce to 110 degrees F and continue to dehydrate for another 4 - 6 hours.
5. Remove from dehydrator and slice. Transfer to serving dish and serve immediately. Or store in airtight container.

Lemon Coconut Biscuits

Prep Time: 5 minutes

Dehydrating Time: 8 - 12 hours

Servings: 12

INGREDIENTS

1 cup cashews

1 cup flaked or shredded coconut

1 lemon

1 tablespoon raw honey

INSTRUCTIONS

1. Add cashews to food processor or high-speed blender and process until finely ground, about 1 minute.
2. Zest *then* juice lemon. Add to processor with coconut and honey. Process until mixture is well combined and sticks together, about 1 - 2 minutes.
3. Line dehydrator trays with dehydrator or parchment sheets.
4. Form mixture into 12 - 24 balls and place on dehydrator or parchment sheets. Press to flatten.
5. Place in dehydrator and dehydrate on 115 degrees F for about 8 - 12 hours, until desired crispiness is reached.
6. Remove from dehydrator and transfer to serving dish. Serve immediately. Or store in airtight container.

Spiced Sesame Chips

Prep Time: 10 minutes
Dehydrating Time: 12 - 20 hours
Servings: 4

INGREDIENTS

- cups ground flax seed
- 1/3 cup whole flax seed
- 1 1/3 cups raw sunflower seeds
- 1/2 cup raw black sesame seeds (or white sesame seeds)
- orange
- teaspoon ground cinnamon
- teaspoon ground ginger
- teaspoon ground black pepper (or ground white pepper)
- teaspoon Celtic sea salt
- 2/3 cups water

INSTRUCTIONS

1. Place parchment paper or dehydrator sheets on dehydrator trays.
2. Zest *then* juice orange and add to large mixing bowl with water, seeds, salt and spices. Mix until well combined.
3. Spread batter on lined dehydrator trays. Place trays in dehydrator and set to 120 degrees F for 1 hour. Reduce temperature to 105 degrees F for 12 - 20.
4. After 4 hours, remove trays from dehydrator and use knife to score crackers in preferred shape and size. Place back in dehydrator and continue dehydrating.

5. Remove trays from dehydrator. Peel crackers from sheets and break apart along score lines. Place crackers directly on dehydrator tray and continue dehydrating another 6 - 12 hours, depending on desired crispness.
6. Remove crackers from dehydrator and serve immediately. Or store in an airtight container.

Cheesy Kale Flax Crackers

Prep Time: 10 minutes

Cook Time: 12 - 24 hours

Servings: 8

INGREDIENTS

2 cups raw almonds

1 kale head (about 3 cups chopped)

1 cup raw coconut flour

1 cup golden flax seed

1 cup water

3/4 cup nutritional yeast

1/2 teaspoon ground black pepper

1 teaspoon smoked paprika

1 teaspoon Celtic sea salt

INSTRUCTIONS

1. Place parchment paper or dehydrator sheets on dehydrator trays.
2. Add flax to food processor or high-speed blender and process until finely ground, about 2 minutes. Transfer to small mixing bowl with water. Mix to combine and set aside.
3. Add almonds to food processor or high-speed blender and process until finely ground, about 2 minutes. Transfer to medium mixing bowl.
4. Wash and spin dry kale. Add to processor and pulse to finely chop, about 1 minute. Add to mixing bowl with nutritional yeast, salt and spices. Add soaked flax and mix until dough forms.

5. Transfer dough to lined dehydrator trays and press into 1/4 inch thick rectangle with hands or rolling pin. Score with knife or pizza cutter into desired shapes.
6. Place tray in dehydrator and dehydrate at 120 degrees F for 2 hours. Reduce temperature to 115 degrees F and continue to dehydrate for 8 - 12 hours.
7. After 6 hours, remove trays from dehydrator and flip crackers. Place back in dehydrator and continue dehydrating .
8. Remove crackers from dehydrator and serve immediately. Or store in airtight container.

Breaded Jalapeño Bites

Prep Time: 20 minutes*

Dehydrating Time: 8 - 24 hours

Servings: 2

INGREDIENTS

6 fresh jalapeño peppers

Filling

1 cup raw sunflower seeds

1/2 cup water

1/4 cup nutritional yeast

1 lemon

1 teaspoon onion powder

1 teaspoon Celtic sea salt

Water

Breading

1/2 cup raw almonds

1/2 teaspoon Celtic sea salt

1/2 teaspoon ground white pepper (or ground black pepper)

1/2 teaspoon garlic powder (optional)

1/2 teaspoon onion powder (optional)

INSTRUCTIONS

1. *Soak sunflower seeds in enough water to cover for 2 hours. Drain and rinse.

2. Cut jalapeños in half lengthwise and remove stems, seeds and veins. Place peppers on dehydrator tray.
3. For *Filling*, juice lemon and add to food processor or high-speed blender with soaked sunflower seeds, water, nutritional yeast, salt, pepper and spices. Process until thick, smooth paste forms, about 2 minutes.
4. Fill piping bag with mixture and pipe into jalapeño halves. Or use teaspoon to scoop filling into jalapeño halves.
5. For *Breading*, add raw almonds to clean food processor orhigh-speed blender with salt and spices. Process until well ground but some texture remains, about 30 seconds.
6. Dip stuffed peppers filling-side down into bread and coat generously.
7. Place stuffed and coated peppers on dehydrator tray filling-side up. Place in dehydrator and dehydrate at 110 degrees F for 8 - 24 hours, depending on desired texture.
8. Remove peppers from dehydrator and serve immediately.

Stuffed Pepperdew Poppers

Prep Time: 15 minutes

Dehydrating Time: 4 - 8 hours

Servings: 2

INGREDIENTS

- 8 pepperdew peppers

Pine Nut Filling

1/4 cup raw tahini (or 6 tablespoons raw sesame seeds)

1/4 cup + 2 tablespoons raw pine nuts

1 tablespoon raw oil (coconut, walnut, almond, sesame, etc.)

1 tablespoon nutritional yeast

Juice of 1/2 lemon

1/2 teaspoon ground white pepper (or ground black pepper)

1/2 teaspoon Celtic sea salt

INSTRUCTIONS

1. Cut tops off of peppers and scoop out seeds. Set aside.
2. Add tahini or sesame seeds, 1/4 cup pine nuts, oil, nutritional yeast, lemon juice, salt and pepper to food processor or high-speed blender. Process until smooth and creamy, up to 5 minutes.
3. Scoop *Pine Nut Filling* into peppers and top with reserved pine nuts. Press pine nuts into stuffing to seal opening.
4. Place filled peppers in dehydrator and dehydrate at 110 degrees F for 4 - 8 hours, until dried but still moist.
5. Remove peppers from dehydrator and transfer to serving dish. Serve immediately. Or store in airtight container.

Berry Granola Bars

Prep Time: 30 minutes

Servings: 8

INGREDIENTS

1 cup raw cashews (or 3/4 cup raw cashew butter)

2 tablespoons flax seed (or chia seed)

1/2 cup dried pitted dates

1/2 cup shredded or flaked coconut

1/3 cup raw pumpkin seeds

1/3 cup raw walnuts

1/3 cup raw almonds

1/4 cup dried cherries

1/4 cup dried blueberries

1/4cup dried raspberries

1/2 teaspoon ground ginger (optional)

1/2 teaspoon vanilla

1 teaspoon Celtic sea salt

INSTRUCTIONS

1. Line loaf pan with parchment paper.
2. Add flax or chia to food processor or high-speed blender and process until finely ground, about 1 - 2 minutes.
3. Add cashews (if using) and process until thick, smooth paste forms, up to 5 minutes.
4. Add dates and process until thick, fairly smooth mixture forms about 1 - 2 minutes. Transfer to medium mixing bowl.

5. Add coconut, pumpkin seeds, walnuts, almonds, vanilla, salt, dried fruit and ginger (optional). Add prepared cashew butter (if using). Stir to combine with large wooden spoon.
6. Transfer mixture to parchment lined pan and firmly press into bottom with hands or spatula. Place in refrigerator for 20 minutes.
7. Remove from refrigerator and cut into bars. Serve chilled. Or allow to warm to room temperature and serve.

Banana Strawberry Leather

Prep Time: 5 minutes

Dehydrating Time: 6 hours

Servings: 6

INGREDIENTS

1 ripe banana

2 cups fresh strawberries (chopped)

2 tablespoons ground chia or flax seed (optional)

Water (optional)

INSTRUCTIONS

1. Remove stems from fresh strawberries and roughly chop. Peel and chop banana. Add to food processor or high-speed blender and process until smooth, about 1 minute.
2. Add ground chia or flax to processor and process with enough water to reach desired consistency. Mixture should be spreadable but not runny.
3. Line dehydrator tray with dehydrator or parchment sheet.
4. Spread mixture on sheet 1/4 inch thick in large rectangle with spatula. Place in dehydrator and dehydrate at 115 degrees F for 4 hours.
5. Remove from dehydrator and use offset spatula to gently peel leather from sheet and flip over. Place back in dehydrator directly on tray and continue to dehydrate for 2 hours.
6. Remove from dehydrator and cut into strips. Or roll up and cut into logs. Transfer to serving dish and serve immediately.

Carrot Crisps

Prep Time: 5 minutes

Dehydrating Time: 18 - 24 hours

Servings: 4

INGREDIENTS

2 large carrots

1 tablespoon raw oil (coconut, walnut, almond, sesame, etc.) (optional)

1/2 teaspoon Celtic sea salt (optional)

INSTRUCTIONS

1. Carefully cut carrot into 1/16 - 1/8 inch thick slices with sharp knife, mandolin or food processor with slicing attachment.
2. Add sliced carrot to medium mixing bowl with oil and salt and toss to coat (optional).
3. Add single layer of sliced carrots to dehydrator tray and place in dehydrator. Dehydrate at 115 degrees F for 12 hours.
4. Remove dehydrator trays and turn over carrot slices. Place trays back in dehydrator and continue dehydrating for 6 - 12 hours, depending on desired crispiness.
5. Remove carrots from dehydrator and transfer to serving dish. Serve immediately. Or store in airtight container.

Crisp Acorn Squash Chips

Prep Time: 5 minutes

Dehydrating Time: 18 - 24 hours

Servings: 4

INGREDIENTS

1 acorn squash

1 tablespoon raw oil (coconut, walnut, almond, sesame, etc.) (optional)

1/4 teaspoon smoked paprika

1/4 teaspoon ground white pepper (or ground black pepper)

1/4 teaspoon Italian seasoning blend (optional)

1/2 teaspoon Celtic sea salt

INSTRUCTIONS

1. Carefully cut acorn squash into 1/16 - 1/8 inch thick slices with sharp knife, mandolin or food processor with slicing attachment.
2. Add sliced squash to medium mixing bowl with oil, salt and spices. Toss to coat.
3. Add single layer of sliced squash to dehydrator tray and place in dehydrator. Dehydrate at 115 degrees F for 12 hours.
4. Remove dehydrator trays and turn over squash slices. Place trays back in dehydrator and continue dehydrating for 6 - 12 hours, depending on desired crispiness.
5. Remove squash from dehydrator and transfer to serving dish. Serve immediately. Or store in airtight container.

Beet Chip Medley

Prep Time: 15 minutes

Dehydrating Time: 18 - 24 hours

Servings: 4

INGREDITENTS

- red beets
- golden beets (or 2 red beets)
- 1/4 cup water
- 1/4 cup raw apple cider vinegar
- tablespoon raw oil (coconut, walnut, almond, sesame, etc.)
- teaspoon Celtic seat salt
- 1/2 teaspoon ground black pepper

INSTRUCTIONS

1. Wash and scrub beets. Carefully cut into 1/16 - 1/8 inch thick slices with sharp knife, mandolin or food processor with slicing attachment.
2. Add sliced beets to medium mixing bowl with water, vinegar and oil. Toss to coat. Set aside 10 minutes.
3. Drain beets, then sprinkle on salt and pepper. Toss to coat.
4. Add single layer of beets to dehydrator tray and place in dehydrator. Dehydrate at 115 degrees F for 12 hours.
5. Remove dehydrator trays and turn over beet slices. Place trays back in dehydrator and continue dehydrating for 12 hours, depending on desired crispiness.
6. Remove beets from dehydrator and transfer to serving dish. Serve immediately. Or store in airtight container.

Dried Mango

Prep Time: 10 minutes

Dehydrating Time: 24 hours

Servings: 4

INGREDIENTS

2 ripe mangos

INSTRUCTIONS

1. Cut mango around pit, and cut into 1/4 inch thick slices. Then remove peel. Or slice then peel.
2. Add single layer of sliced mango to dehydrator trays. Place in dehydrator and dehydrate at 115 degrees F for 24 hours, or until dried but not crisp.
3. Remove mango from dehydrator and transfer to serving dish. Serve immediately. Or store in airtight container.

Primal Pineapple Strips

Prep Time: 10 minutes

Dehydrating Time: 12 - 16 hours

Servings: 4

INGREDIENTS

1 ripe pineapple

INSTRUCTIONS

1. Peel pineapple and cut around core into 1/4 - 1/3 inch thick slices.
2. Add single layer of sliced pineapple to dehydrator trays. Place in dehydrator and dehydrate at 115 degrees F for 12 - 16 hours, or until dried but not crisp.
3. Remove pineapple from dehydrator and transfer to serving dish. Serve immediately. Or store in airtight container.

Crisp Banana Chips

Prep Time: 5 minutes

Dehydrating Time: 12 - 16 hours

Servings: 4

INGREDIENTS

4 ripe or overripe bananas

INSTRUCTIONS
1. Peel bananas and cut into 1/4 - 1/3 inch thick slices lengthwise or crosswise.
2. Line dehydrator trays with dehydrator or parchment sheet. Add single layer of sliced banana to lined dehydrator trays .
3. Place bananas in dehydrator and dehydrate on 115 degrees F for 12 - 16 hours, depending on desired crispiness.
4. Remove bananas from dehydrator and transfer to serving dish. Serve immediately. Or store in airtight container.

Crisp Apple Chips

Prep Time: 5 minutes

Dehydrating Time: 10 - 14 hours

Servings: 4

INGREDIENTS

4 sweet apples

1 teaspoon ground cinnamon (optional)

INSTRUCTIONS

1. Carefully cut apple around core into 1/16 - 1/8 inch thick slices with sharp knife, mandolin or food processor with slicing attachment.
2. Add single layer of sliced apple to dehydrator tray . Sprinkle with cinnamon (optional). Place in dehydrator and dehydrate at 105 degrees F for 10 - 14 hours, depending on desired crispiness.
3. Remove apples from dehydrator and transfer to serving dish. Serve immediately. Or store in airtight container.

Spiced Kale Chips

Prep Time: 10 minutes

Dehydrating Time: 4 - 6 hours

Servings: 4

INGREDIENTS

2 kale heads (or 1.5 - 2 lbs kale leaves)

3 tablespoons raw oil (coconut, walnut, almond, sesame, etc.)

1 tablespoon coconut aminos (or tamari, apple cider vinegar or lemon juice)

1/2 teaspoon smoked paprika

1 teaspoon cayenne pepper

1 teaspoon ground black pepper

1 teaspoon Celtic sea salt

INSTRUCTIONS

1. Wash and spin dry kale. Remove tough spine and chop or tear into pieces.
2. Add kale pieces to large mixing bowl with oil, vinegar salt and spices. Toss to coat.
3. Add single layer of coated kale to dehydrator tray and place in dehydrator. Dehydrate at 115 degrees F for 4 - 6 hours, depending on desired crispiness.
4. Remove kale from dehydrator and transfer to serving dish. Serve immediately. Or store in airtight container.

Sweet Potato Crisps

Prep Time: 5 minutes
Dehydrating Time: 24 hours
Servings: 4

INGREDIENTS

- large sweet potato
- tablespoons raw oil (coconut, walnut, almond, sesame, etc.)
- teaspoon Celtic sea salt
- 1/2 teaspoon ground black pepper (optional)

INSTRUCTIONS

1. Carefully cut sweet potato into 1/16 - 1/8 inch thick slices with sharp knife, mandolin or food processor with slicing attachment.
2. Add sliced sweet potato to medium mixing bowl with oil, salt and pepper. Toss to coat.
3. Add single layer of coated sweet potatoes to dehydrator tray and place in dehydrator. Dehydrate at 115 degrees F for 12 hours.
4. Remove dehydrator trays and turn over sweet potato slices. Place trays back in dehydrator and continue dehydrating for about 12 hours, depending on desired crispiness.
5. Remove sweet potatoes from dehydrator and transfer to serving dish. Serve immediately. Or store in airtight container.

Cheesy Veggie Popcorn

Prep Time: 5 minutes

Dehydrating Time: 12 - 24 hours

Servings: 2

INGREDIENTS

2 cups cauliflower florets (roughly chopped)

1 teaspoon raw oil (coconut, walnuts, almond, sesame, etc.)

1 teaspoon coconut aminos (or tamari, apple cider vinegar or lemon juice)

3 tablespoons nutritional yeast

1 teaspoon Celtic sea salt

INSTRUCTIONS

1. Cut larger cauliflower florets into smaller pieces. Add to medium mixing bowl or container with well-fitting lid.
2. Evenly sprinkle on oil, coconut aminos, nutritional yeast and salt.
3. Secure lid on bowl or container and shake well until cauliflower is evenly coated.
4. Line dehydrator trays with dehydrator or parchment sheets.
5. Add single layer of coated cauliflower to lined dehydrator trays and place in dehydrator. Dehydrate at 115 degrees F for 12 - 24 hours, until desired crispiness is reached. Turn cauliflower over half way through dehydrating.
6. Remove from dehydrator and transfer to serving dish. Serve immediately.

Made in United States
North Haven, CT
04 November 2022